States

OREGON

by Tyler Maine

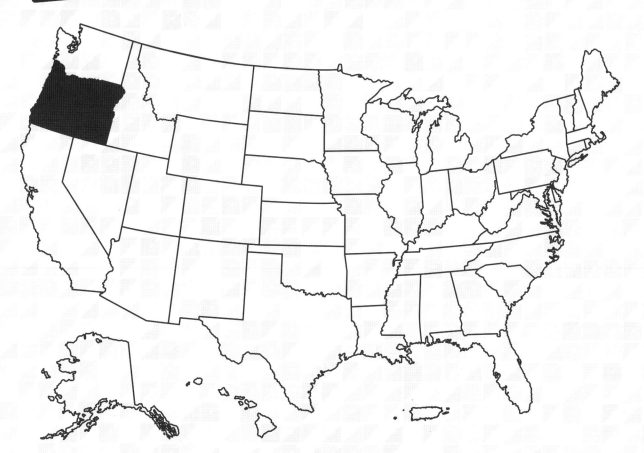

CAPSTONE PRESS
a capstone imprint

Next Page Books are published by Capstone Press,
1710 Roe Crest Drive, North Mankato, Minnesota 56003
www.mycapstone.com

Library of Congress Cataloging-in-Publication Data
Cataloging-in-publication information is on file with the Library of
Congress.
ISBN 978-1-5157-0424-9 (library binding)
ISBN 978-1-5157-0483-6 (paperback)
ISBN 978-1-5157-0535-2 (ebook PDF)

Editorial Credits
Jaclyn Jaycox, editor; Kazuko Collins and Katy LaVigne, designers;
Morgan Walters, media researcher; Tori Abraham, production specialist

Photo Credits
Alamy: nsf, 28; Capstone Press: Angi Gahler, map 4, 7; CriaImages.
com: Jay Robert Nash Collection, top 18, top 19; Getty Images: Archive
Photos/MPI, bottom 19, Time & Life Pictures/Terry Smith, middle 18;
Globe Photos: M. Berkley, middle 19; Newscom: Ingram Publishing, 27,
Michael Goulding/ZUMAPRESS, 29; North Wind Picture Archives, 12,
25, 26; One Mile Up, Inc., flag, seal 23; Shutterstock: Atmosphere1, 16,
Checubus, bottom 24, Freebilly, 11, grafvision, 14, Imfoto, top left 21,
Jody Ann, middle right 21, Josemaria Toscano, cover, 5, JPL Designs,
13, kan_khampanya, bottom left 8, LifetimeStock, top 24, Lori Howard,
top left 20, LorraineHudgins, bottom left 21, M.Khebra, bottom right
20, Melisa Claridad, bottom right 8, Robert Bohrer, 10, s_bukley,
bottom 18, schankz, bottom right 21, Sombra, top right 20, Sung Choi,
6, TFoxFoto, 15, Tom Reichner, bottom left 20, tusharkoley, 9, 17,
zschnepf, 7; Wikimedia: David Rix Eibonvale, top right 21, National
Oceanic and Atmospheric Administration, middle left 21

All design elements by Shutterstock

Printed and bound in China.
0316/CA21600187
012016 009436F16

TABLE OF CONTENTS

Want to take your research further? Ask your librarian if your school subscribes to PebbleGo Next. If so, when you see this helpful symbol (↖) throughout the book, log onto www.pebblegonext.com for bonus downloads and information.

LOCATION

Oregon is in the northwestern United States. Washington borders Oregon to the north. The Pacific Ocean crashes along Oregon's western coast. California and Nevada lie south of Oregon. Idaho lies east of Oregon. The Coast Range mountains run along the coast. They give Oregon a rugged, rocky coastline. East of the Coast Range is the Cascade Range. The wide Willamette Valley lies between these two mountain ranges. Dense forests cover about half of Oregon. Portland, Eugene, and Salem are the state's largest cities. Salem is Oregon's capital.

PebbleGo Next Bonus!
To print and label
your own map, go to
www.pebblegonext.com
and search keywords:
OR MAP

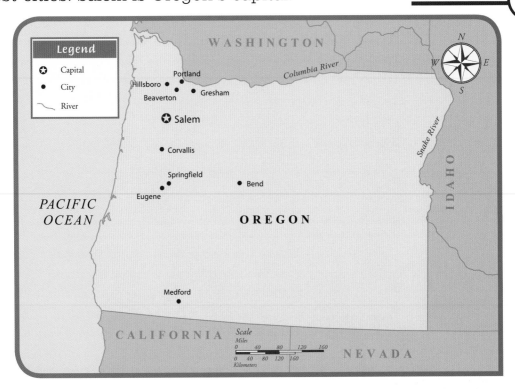

Portland's name was chosen in 1845 by the flip of a coin. Had the coin flipped the other way, it would've been named Boston.

GEOGRAPHY

Oregon's Pacific Coast has sandy beaches and rocky cliffs. Tree-covered mountain ranges rise in the western part of the state. Also in the west, the Willamette River gives life to rich farmland. Oregon's Cascade Mountains have many volcanic peaks, including Mount Hood, the tallest peak in the state. It rises to 11,239 feet (3,426 meters) above sea level. East of the Cascade Mountains lies the Columbia Plateau.

PebbleGo Next Bonus! To watch a video about the end of the Oregon Trail and the murals in Vale, go to www.pebblegonext.com and search keywords:

OR VIDEO

There are more than 80 state parks and recreation areas along the 363-mile- (584-kilometer-) long Oregon Coast.

The Three Sisters are three tall peaks located in the Cascade Mountains.

Legend

▲ Highest Point
⬮ Lake
🝔 Mountain Range
▢ National Park
⬭ Point of Interest
〰 River

COASTAL REGION

COAST RANGE

WILLAMETTE VALLEY

Willamette River

CASCADE MOUNTAINS

Columbia River

John Day River

BLUE MOUNTAINS

Snake River

Mount Hood

Deschutes River

WALLOWA MOUNTAINS

Hells Canyon

COLUMBIA

PLATEAU

KLAMATH MOUNTAINS

Crater Lake

CRATER LAKE NATIONAL PARK

Malheur Lake

BASIN AND

RANGE REGION

Rogue River

Upper Klamath Lake

PACIFIC OCEAN

Scale
Miles
0   40   80   120

0   40   80   120
Kilometers

WEATHER

Summers and winters are mild in western Oregon. Temperatures in eastern Oregon are more extreme. In winter temperatures in this region may dip below 0 degrees Fahrenheit (minus 18 degrees Celsius). Summer temperatures in eastern Oregon usually reach above 90°F (32°C).

Average High and Low Temperatures (Salem, OR)

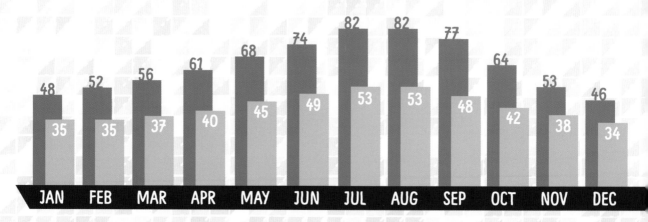

	JAN	FEB	MAR	APR	MAY	JUN	JUL	AUG	SEP	OCT	NOV	DEC
High	48	52	56	61	68	74	82	82	77	64	53	46
Low	35	35	37	40	45	49	53	53	48	42	38	34

Mount Hood

Mount Hood, Oregon's highest peak, is a volcano. But it's not expected to erupt. It's a dormant, or "sleeping," volcano. However, tremors are often felt in the ground there.

Crater Lake National Park

At 1,950 feet (594 m) deep, Crater Lake in southwestern Oregon is the deepest lake in the United States. It is the seventh-deepest lake in the world. It formed after a huge volcano erupted.

Multnomah Falls

Multnomah Falls is a famous place in the Columbia River Gorge. At 620 feet (189 m) high, it is the highest waterfall in the state.

HISTORY AND GOVERNMENT

The terrain of the Oregon Trail was often difficult for settlers to cross.

Long before white settlers arrived, American Indians lived in Oregon. In 1792 American explorer Captain Robert Gray sailed up the Columbia River. In 1805 the Lewis and Clark Expedition reached the Pacific Ocean by traveling through Oregon. Fur traders then traveled to Oregon. They sent news back to the east about Oregon's rich resources. In the mid-1800s, thousands of settlers then poured into Oregon from eastern states. Many came on a covered wagon route called the Oregon Trail. In 1848 the United States created Oregon Territory. Oregon became the 33rd state in 1859.

Oregon's government is divided into three branches. The legislative branch makes laws. It has a 30-member Senate and a 60-member House of Representatives. The executive branch, led by the governor, makes sure people obey state laws. The judicial branch decides whether a law has been broken.

Oregon's first two capitol buildings were destroyed by fires in 1855 and 1935.

INDUSTRY

One of Oregon's largest industries is forestry. Oregon wood becomes logs, boards, cardboard, and paper products. Oregon requires landowners to replant trees after a timber harvest.

Agriculture accounts for one-fifth of Oregon's economy. Oregon is the nation's top producer of Christmas trees, hazelnuts, grass seed, peppermint, black raspberries, and blackberries.

Making high-technology products is a large part of Oregon's manufacturing industry. Computer companies Hewlett-Packard and Intel have factories in Oregon's Willamette Valley.

The Willamette Valley produces 99 percent of the country's hazelnuts.

Tourism has become a big business in Oregon. Tourists ski, hike, bike, boat, mountain climb, fish, and camp in Oregon's many wilderness areas. Sport and commercial fishing is very popular in Oregon. The state is famous for its river salmon.

Douglas-fir and ponderosa pine trees are the most important to Oregon's timber industry.

POPULATION

Most Oregonians have European backgrounds. Many of their ancestors came from England, Switzerland, Ireland, Scotland, Germany, Poland, and Italy. Some of these early settlers came from the eastern United States over the Oregon Trail.

Hispanic Americans are Oregon's second-largest ethnic group. Most Hispanic Americans in Oregon have Mexican backgrounds. Large populations of Hispanic Americans live in Portland and Salem.

Chinese, Japanese, and Filipino immigrants came to the state in the late 1800s and early 1900s. They worked on the railroads and in canneries. Portland and Beaverton are home to the state's largest populations of Asian Americans.

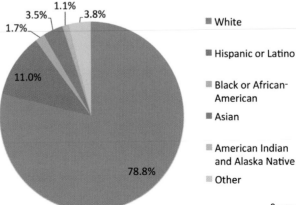

Population by Ethnicity

- 3.5%
- 1.7%
- 1.1%
- 3.8%
- 11.0%
- 78.8%

- White
- Hispanic or Latino
- Black or African-American
- Asian
- American Indian and Alaska Native
- Other

Source: U.S. Census Bureau.

FAMOUS PEOPLE

Chief Joseph (circa 1840–1904) was a Nez Perce chief. White settlers and the U.S. Army forced his people out of Oregon. Then he led them on a long trek through Idaho and Montana, where they were captured and forced onto a reservation.

Beverly Cleary (1916–) is an award-winning author of children's books. Her books include *Henry Higgins* (1950), *Ramona the Pest* (1968), and *Dear Mr. Henshaw* (1983).

Matt Groening (1954–) is the cartoonist who created the Simpsons. He named the characters after his own family members.

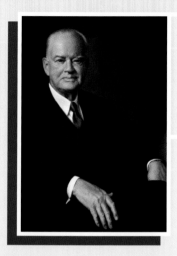

Herbert Hoover (1874–1964) was the 31st president of the United States (1929–1933). He was born in Iowa and grew up in Newberg.

Ursula Le Guin (1929–) is the author of many science fiction books. She was born in California and settled in Portland.

John McLoughlin (1784–1857) is called the "Father of Oregon." Born in Canada, he helped settle the Oregon Territory.

STATE SYMBOLS

Tree

Douglas fir

Flower

Oregon grape

Bird

western meadowlark

Fish

Chinook salmon

PebbleGo Next Bonus! To make a dessert using one of Oregon's highly produced fruits, go to www.pebblegonext.com and search keywords:

OR RECIPE

Gemstone

Oregon sunstone

Rock

thunder egg (geode)

Seashell

Oregon hairy triton (conch)

Animal

beaver

Insect

swallowtail butterfly

Nut

hazelnut

FAST FACTS

STATEHOOD
1859

CAPITAL ☆
Salem

LARGEST CITY •
Portland

SIZE
95,988 square miles (248,608 square kilometers) land area (2010 U.S. Census Bureau)

POPULATION
3,930,065 (2013 U.S. Census estimate)

STATE NICKNAME
Beaver State

STATE MOTTO
"She flies with her own wings"

STATE SEAL

Oregon's state seal has a shield bordered by 33 stars. The shield is divided by a ribbon that reads, "The Union." Above the ribbon are the mountains and forests of Oregon. A covered wagon and a team of oxen stand for the settlers who came to Oregon. A British ship is shown leaving, while an American ship arrives. Below the shield is a sheaf of wheat, a plow, and a pickax, which all represent the state's agriculture. Above the shield is the American eagle.

PebbleGo Next Bonus! To print and color your own flag, go to www.pebblegonext.com and search keywords:

OR FLAG

STATE FLAG

The Oregon state flag is blue with gold lettering and symbols. Blue and gold are the state's colors. The shield is surrounded by 33 stars. Above the shield are the words "State of Oregon." Below the shield, the date of statehood, 1859, is written. On the reverse side of the flag is a beaver, the state animal. Oregon is the only U.S. state that has a different pattern on the back of the flag. The Oregon state flag was adopted in 1925.

MINING PRODUCTS

crushed stone, sand and gravel, clays

MANUFACTURED GOODS

computer and electronic equipment, food products, wood products

To learn the lyrics to the state song, go to www.pebblegonext.com and search keywords:

OR SONG

FARM PRODUCTS

greenhouse and nursery products, Christmas trees, hazelnuts, wheat, hay, berries

PROFESSIONAL SPORTS TEAMS

Portland Trail Blazers (NBA)
Portland Timbers (MLS)

OREGON TIMELINE

1500s About 100 American Indian tribes live in Oregon.

1620 The Pilgrims establish a colony in the New World in present-day Massachusetts.

1792 Captain Robert Gray sails into the Columbia River and names the river after his ship.

1805 On November 7 explorers Lewis and Clark reach the Pacific Ocean at the mouth of the Columbia River.

1848 Oregon Territory is created.

1840–1860
More than 300,000 settlers travel the Oregon Trail.

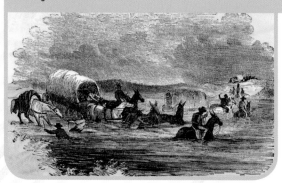

1859
On February 14 Oregon becomes the 33rd state.

1861–1865
The Union and the Confederacy fight the Civil War.

1877
U.S. troops battle the Nez Perce Indians; the Nez Perce surrender in Montana.

1902 On May 22 Crater Lake National Park becomes Oregon's only national park.

1914–1918 World War I is fought; the United States enters the war in 1917.

1922 Columbia River Scenic Highway is completed on June 27. It is the first paved highway in the northwestern United States.

1938 Bonneville Dam on the Columbia River is completed.

1939–1945 World War II is fought; the United States enters the war in 1941.

1942 A Japanese submarine fires at Fort Stevens, in northwestern Oregon, in one of the only attacks on the U.S. mainland in World War II.

1966 On August 27 the Astoria Bridge opens over the Columbia River, linking Oregon and Washington.

1960s & 1970s Oregon's government passes many laws to reduce pollution and clean up the environment.

1980
On May 18 Mount St. Helens in Washington erupts, spewing clouds of volcanic ash across Oregon and much of the Pacific Northwest.

2002
A record forest fire season in Oregon burns more than 1 million acres (405,000 hectares).

2009
Oregon celebrates 150 years of statehood.

2012
The University of Oregon Ducks win their first Rose Bowl football game in 95 years.

2015
Oregon becomes the second state to offer free community college to students graduating high school; this program is called the "Oregon Promise."

Glossary

ancestor *(AN-ses-tuhr)*—a member of a person's family who lived a long time ago

ethnic *(ETH-nik)*—related to a group of people and their culture

executive *(ig-ZE-kyuh-tiv)*—the branch of government that makes sure laws are followed

immigrant *(IM-uh-gruhnt)*—someone who comes from abroad to live permanently in a country

industry *(IN-duh-stree)*—a business which produces a product or provides a service

judicial *(joo-DISH-uhl)*—to do with the branch of government that explains and interprets the laws

legislature *(LEJ-iss-lay-chur)*—a group of elected officials who have the power to make or change laws for a country or state

region *(REE-juhn)*—a large area

reservation *(rez-er-VAY-shuhn)*—an area of land set aside by the U.S. government for American Indians

surrender *(suh-REN-dur)*—to give up or admit defeat

tremor *(TREM-ur)*—a shaking or trembling movement

Read More

Bjorklund, Ruth. *Oregon: The Beaver State.* It's My State! New York: Cavendish Square Publishing, 2016.

Felix, Rebecca. *What's Great About Oregon?* Our Great States. Minneapolis: Lerner Publications Company, 2015.

Ganeri, Anita. *United States of America: A Benjamin Blog and His Inquisitive Dog Guide.* Country Guides. Chicago: Heinemann Raintree, 2015.

Internet Sites

FactHound offers a safe, fun way to find Internet sites related to this book. All of the sites on FactHound have been researched by our staff.

Here's all you do:

Visit *www.facthound.com*

Type in this code: 9781515704249

Check out projects, games and lots more at
www.capstonekids.com

Critical Thinking Using the Common Core

1. Forestry is one of Oregon's largest industries. What does Oregon wood become? (Key Ideas and Details)

2. What was the Oregon Trail? (Key Ideas and Details)

3. Mount Hood is not expected to erupt. It is a dormant volcano, but tremors are still often felt. What is a tremor? (Craft and Structure)

Index